PRACTICING INCLUSIVITY

A Workbook for Transformation

by

Shariff Abdullah

With Leslie Hamilton

PRACTICING INCLUSIVITY

Commonway Publishing

P. O. Box 12541

Portland, OR 97212

permissions@commonway.org

publisher@commonway.org

Ordering Information:

This book may be ordered directly from www.amazon.com.

Quantity sales. Special discounts are available on quantity purchases by organizations, associations, and others. For details, contact the publisher at the address above.

Printed in the United States of America

Second Printing (Ver. 2.2), 2016

ISBN: 978-1517347819

Grammatical Note: In 2015, in order to connect more closely with his ancestors, and to improve the overall numerology, Shariff made a slight change to his name: from Sharif Mujahid Abdullah to Shariff Moore Abdullah. In this text, when referring to his publications that were published before 2015, "Sharif" (with one "f") will be used. This is intentional.

Editing and formatting by Constellations Concept & Copy, www.Constellations.biz.

TABLE OF CONTENTS

FOREWORD

In our society, we find it difficult to address our differences. Differences in race, class and culture, differences in ideology and point of view, differences in language, gender or sexual orientation ... all can contribute to miscommunication, reduced productivity, personal stress, discrimination and conflict.

In our society, we practice exclusivity, the world-view of "I am separate from you." I can treat you well; I can treat you poorly—it doesn't matter because nothing comes back to me. The world-view of exclusivity is the basis behind all of the -isms that we have in our society, *e.g.* racism, sexism, homophobia, etc.

We have attempted to resolve these important issues, like racism or sexism, without first addressing the underlying concept and world-view of exclusivity. It has not worked. It does not work. We have no reason to believe that it will work in the future. Applying a flawed concept with more vigor does not make the flaw go away.

If we intend to move beyond the presenting surface issues, if we intend to actually resolve our exclusivist challenges, we must first understand and practice the principles of inclusivity.

Inclusivity is the notion that we are all connected. We are inextricably linked to each other. Our connections go beyond "liking" or "tolerating" each other. Inclusivity is the world-view that all beings are connected. Inclusivity can be summed up in the statement, "We Are One."

Inclusivity is not just a feeling. Inclusivity is a perspective. It's the way you choose to interact with the world. It is something that you PRACTICE. And, like any other practice, it is something that you never achieve but are constantly striving to improve.

So, we invite you to start your journey with us right here and now.

Shariff M. Abdullah

Leslie Hamilton

Outcomes:

- To understand the basic concepts of Inclusivity.

- To understand the purpose of this course.

- To prepare for your learning experience.

"Do unto others as you would have them do unto you.
I mean, REALLY."
—Shariff Abdullah

MEDITATION
Start with a 5-10 minute meditation.
Record your beginning attitudes
and initial impressions in your journal.

"Do unto others as you would have them do unto you.
I mean, REALLY."
—Shariff Abdullah

1.1 The Golden Rule

We refer to the above quote as the Golden Rule. While that phraseology is based in Christianity, there are similar expressions of inclusivity in all other major wisdom traditions.

What is hateful to you, do not do to others. (Judaism)

[The real saint] looks impartial on all—lover, friend or foe; indifferent or hostile; alien or relative; virtuous or sinful. (Hinduism)

Do not hurt others with that which hurts yourself. (Buddhism)

Do unto others whatever you would have them do unto you. (Christianity)

None of you is a believer until you love for your neighbor what you love for yourself. (Islam)

Without the flowery language, all these tenets mean the same thing: treat others the way you want to be treated. For the purposes of this course, the term Golden Rule refers to this concept even though many other religions, cultures and wisdom traditions use other terms to describe it. This is for simplicity—not to demean or promote any particular expression of this universal truth.

The purpose of this course is to teach the practice of inclusivity even in the most difficult circumstances we can imagine: even with the Other. The Other is the person we feel compelled to reject or part ways from, the person we believe might attack us psychologically, emotionally or even physically (more on this in Chapter 4).

The origins of the Golden Rule go even deeper—down into the wisdom teachings of indigenous cultures. The Golden Rule may be our most basic and widely shared human value. It is also the most uniformly ignored human value. And it is the Golden Rule that forms the basis of inclusivity.

EXERCISE: **The Golden Rule**

Reflect on the following questions. Explore your attitude, beliefs and assumptions about the Golden Rule. Record your thoughts and insights in your journal.

1. Did you grow up with a knowledge or understanding of the Golden Rule (from your own spiritual/cultural background)?

2. Were you encouraged to practice it?

3. Who did you see practicing it?

4. From your culture/community experience when you were growing up, who (if anyone) was excluded, "Other"?

5. When you were growing up, how did your family/ friends refer to "The Other" (people who were different – race, ethnicity, culture, language, religion, etc.)? Positively? Negatively? Not at all?

6. Do you practice the Golden Rule now? How?

7. If you don't, what prevents you?

8. In what situations is it challenging? Easy?

9. Do you think that practicing inclusivity is important? Why? Why not?

1.2 About "Practicing Inclusivity"

The purpose of this course is not to convince you that the Golden Rule is a good idea. It's likely you already believe that it is. The purpose of this course is to teach you how to practice inclusivity, even in the most difficult circumstances you can imagine: practicing with the Other.

The inspiration to practice inclusivity is not just because we believe it is the right thing to do, but because our society is in turmoil and the practice of Inclusivity is a way out. The living practice of the Principle of Inclusivity can heal all societal dysfunctions. (A bold statement! We hope to deliver!) We practice inclusivity not because it's a "good idea," but because practicing exclusivity is social and spiritual suicide.

The goal of this course on inclusivity is to have all of us, including adversaries, recognize that we depend on each other. In this way, we can create a global human community.

Although you are embarking on an individually based learning experience, the COURSE IS BEST WHEN DONE WITH OTHERS (not in isolation). The inquiry into our values and our practices is best done in the context of working with others. Therefore, along with your reading and exercises, there will be exercises that require you to involve others. This will enable you to deepen and practice your understanding of inclusivity, and thereby, transform society.

1.3 Preparing for the Course Experience

The learning process you are embarking upon is a combination of meditating, reading, reflecting, contemplation, sharing, taking action and creating results. The course is carefully designed to provide an integrated experience to maximize the results you gain.

Take the time you need to complete the lessons and actions. At the same time, stay focused, motivated and committed to your learning. Your level of engagement and focus will determine the results you create.

EXERCISE: My Motivation, Purpose & Goals

Reflect on the following questions in order to specify your <u>motivation</u>, <u>purpose</u> and <u>desired outcomes</u> for your learning experience. Record your thoughts in your journal.

1. What is it that you want to create? What motivates you to act?

2. Why is that creating important to you?

3. How will you know when you have it? (What will you see? Hear? Be doing? Be telling yourself? Feeling?)

4. When, where and with whom to do you want it? When, where and with whom do you NOT want it?

5. What are your resources?

6. What will be better? Worse?

7. What drives you to make this happen?

8. What causes you to lose motivation or focus?

9. How will your life be significantly different when you have achieved your goal?

1.4 Increasing Your Awareness of Yourself

Throughout the course, you'll be developing new understanding and insights about yourself and others.

Take note of how this new information can help you change your behaviors, beliefs, attitudes and assumptions.

 EXERCISE: **The Hand Exercise**

1. On a blank piece of paper, trace your dominant hand.

2. On a second piece of paper, trace your non-dominant hand.

3. On each finger of your dominant hand, write one positive personal trait, something that you appreciate about yourself. What are your personal characteristics that will contribute to your successful completion of this course?

4. On each finger of your non-dominant hand, write a negative, challenging or non-constructive personality trait you feel you might need to curb or control. What are your personal characteristics that may interfere with your successful completion of this course?

After you complete this exercise, share your drawings with your others. Share your thoughts about the following questions:

1. How do my positive traits help me be successful in my life? How have I used these traits over time?

2. How do my non-constructive traits get in the way of my success? How have I balanced or eliminated them over time?

3. How are my constructive and non-constructive traits similar and different? (Many times, these traits are two sides of the same coin ... positive or negative only in degree.)

4. How can I use my understanding of my own traits to understand others better?

5. Ask others if they see different traits in you than you see in yourself.

1.5 Incorporate Your Spiritual Practices into Your Learning

The practice of inclusivity is linked to spiritual practice. (Remember: Spiritual does not mean religious.) To assist you in experiencing this connection, every chapter begins and ends with a meditation. When starting the meditations, find a quiet, comfortable place, position your body in an alert and relaxed state. (Lying down is not recommended. You should be positioned and located so that you do not have to do much position changing in order to start your course study. Also, lying down can encourage sleeping.)

If you have an established spiritual practice, you may prefer to use your own process or incorporate the course meditations into your own process.

If you do not already have an established meditation practice, the course meditations will provide you with all the direction you need to use them as a learning tool for this course.

Don't skimp! Because of the close link between inclusivity and spirituality, it is important that you do the meditation before you begin each chapter and when you complete each chapter. It is also recommended that you participate in the opening and closing meditation at the beginning and end of each group study session, if you are studying with others.

1.6 Create Time and Space

Create a regularly scheduled time for you to engage in the course. Leaving it to the in-between or free time, or when you "get around to it" may make it difficult for you to maintain your momentum. Creating a regularly scheduled time for you to engage in the course is telling yourself that the course is important.

Find a place that provides the environment where you can concentrate as well as have access to the resources you need for the learning at hand. (Not in front of the TV or in the kids' playing area.)

Inclusive Action: Engage with a Practice Group

Engaging with others will deeply enhance your learning and help you stay accountable to your learning. Your "group" may be one other person. Your group will:

1. Help you stay on schedule and engage regularly with the learning material.

2. Listen to you explain the concepts you are learning.

3. Be reliable, open and honest, challenging and holding yourself accountable to your learning.

4. Share viewpoints and opinions or play devil's advocate to help you explore the boundaries of your thinking, experience and learning.

Inclusive Action: How to Form a Practice Group

The best practice group practices with others who are taking the course. This will ensure that all group members have a similar motivation for staying on task and completing the course. And, this will help you engage with the materials as both a participant and a facilitator.

Organize a practice group at your church or religious organization's meeting place, or with a social club or organization. Consider a brown-bag practice group at your job.

If you cannot arrange to practice with people taking the Course, have two to three good friends who will commit to working with you. (Please remember: this is copyrighted material. Your practice group is not authorized to receive the Inclusivity materials unless they have paid for it.)

It may be possible to arrange a virtual practice group if there are a number of participants who cannot find practice partners.

Experiences of past participants verify that merely reading the exercises without actually engaging and completing them greatly diminishes the learning and value they gained from the course. "Thinking" an answer in your head, or "imagining" an engagement is not the same as actually doing the exercise.

EXERCISE: Organize Your Time, Space and Materials

1. Decide when you'll be at your best to do your course.

- A Regular Schedule: What time of day will work best for you to focus on your course? What days of the week work best for you? Have a regular and consistent time and day to engage in the materials. Don't try to "fit it in" between scheduled events. Make THIS a scheduled event!

- A Regular Place: Decide where you want to be when you're engaging with the course material. Have a consistent place for learning. And, once established, make your space "off limits" during your course time. If you are studying with a group, make it a priority to be prompt, to be prepared, to participate in the group meditation and to otherwise be present for the group.

2. Have the Required Resources

- Journal: Reflection is a key part of the learning process. Having a journal to record your reflections and thoughts is important to enhance your learning and provide a reference and refresher tool. If you are using a printed version of the workbook, please use the white space as your journal to create a personalized version for yourself.

- Computer and Internet Access: Some of you will be accessing this course via the Web. Even for those accessing via printed materials, some lessons use web-based media so you will need computer access.

LEARNING DISCUSSION OF CHAPTER ONE

Consult your journal before answering these questions:

For Each Section:

- What was one thing you agreed with?

- What was one thing you didn't understand, or you disagreed with?

For Each Exercise:

- What was your experience of the exercise?

- What did you learn? What will you take away?

- What did you find unclear or difficult?

For the Chapter:

- What was your strongest take-away from this chapter?

- What was your most difficult or challenging concept to practice?

- What was the most interesting thing you wrote after your meditation?

> MEDITATION
> Reflections on Your Personal Journey
> Conclude this chapter with a five- to ten-minute
> meditation. Record your reflections in your
> journal or below.

Outcomes:

- To understand the *Philosophy of Inclusivity*.

- To recognize factors that inhibit inclusivity.

- To see and advocate for the whole.

*... Our greatest strength lies not in how much we differ
from each other, but in how much—
how very much—we are the same.*

—Eknath Easwaran

MEDITATION
Start with a 5-10 minute meditation.
Record your beginning attitudes
and initial impressions in your journal.

... Our greatest strength lies not in how much we differ from each other, but in how much— how very much—we are the same.

—Eknath Easwaran

2.1 Overview of the Philosophy

The *Philosophy of Inclusivity* is deeply rooted in our wisdom traditions and is also aligned with our practical common future. Simply put, **inclusivity is the concept that each of our lives is inextricably linked to each other.** It is the essence of what has been called *The Golden Rule.*

Inclusivity is NOT:
- Conflict resolution, although it involves resolving conflict.

- Just compromising or balancing competing factors.

- Inclusion, inclusiveness or any other concept that involves including historically excluded groups— although such groups are definitely a part of inclusivity.

- Part of any theory based on excluding or separating from any group.

- Finding a middle ground between opposing or disagreeing parties.

Inclusivity IS:
- A primary human value.

- Perceiving from a different point of view.

- Recognizing that building relationships is more important than solving a problem.

- Taking a position that is larger than the advocacy or achievement of the parts.

- Transcending exclusivist relationships.

- Creating common ground.

Inclusivity means we can experience connection, interaction and community with everyone, including potential adversaries. In practicing inclusivity, we must be vigilant not to support or encourage one side or factor over another, regardless of our personal affinity or revulsion. Getting labeled as a partisan reduces one's effectiveness to bring people together.

Inclusivity means we can be in the presence of our potential adversaries and have meaningful interactions with them.

Remember: you and your group are seen as "Other" or as an adversary to some group. Our goal is to have all people, all BEINGS, recognize that they depend on each other, that each and every action (and non-action) reverberates throughout the community— indeed, the world. My fate is linked with yours. That is the essence of inclusivity.

We define community as EVERYONE who lives or has authentic interests in a given area. Because this is how we define our stakeholders, our goal is also to help people develop a sense of community.

2.2 The Challenge of Inclusivity

For the first time, human technology has advanced to a point where it is possible for every human being to be aware of and in contact with every other human being. We are a phone call away from every major city, on every continent, as well as most towns and villages—even the South Pole. For the first time, the affairs of humans span the globe and span every culture.

Paradoxically, this is also the time when the human family has experienced the deepest conflict with itself. Our enhanced ability to communicate gives us greater opportunities to communicate our prejudices, pains and fears. We are challenged by fear-damaged human beings acting out of their fear. We ourselves are fearful and act out of that fear.

There are more than 70 wars raging on our planet right now, and, unless we learn to practice inclusivity, the number is destined to go up, not down. The overt reason for these wars and conflicts is the FEAR OF DIFFERENCE AND LOSS.

Some of the 70 global wars and violent conflicts are based on religious difference: Muslims and Christians battle in Eastern Europe and the Philippines; Muslims and Jews in the Middle East; Buddhists and Hindus in Sri Lanka; Catholics and Protestants in Northern Ireland. Some of the wars are based on ethnic/racial difference: conflicts in Southern Africa (Rwanda, for example) and the southern part of North America pit white-skinned people against black-skinned people. Some of these wars are based on a quest to obtain or maintain power and wealth: Syria and Zimbabwe are current examples. The aftereffects of these conflicts will be with us for decades. Unless we do something about it, they will continue for generations.

Wherever people feel threatened by change, the philosophy of Inclusivity is necessary. Regardless of the specific issue, the real issue is always the same. It can come in the form of: "I am afraid of change;" "I am afraid of losing my identity;" "I am afraid of you;" "I am afraid for my well-being and for the well-being of my family;" or "I am afraid of losing power or control." The core issue is "I am afraid."

What do you do when you are afraid? Most of us shut down and shut other people out. Others lash-out or attack. Neither "fight" nor "flight" is an adequate response in the 21st Century. The *Philosophy of Inclusivity* changes that dynamic to being open and inviting.

We are asked to be compassionate with people we find reprehensible. It works both ways: those people look at you and find you reprehensible as well. Your compassion toward them can help them see a different world. They can help you see differently, too.

Wherever people feel threatened, the *Philosophy of Inclusivity* is necessary. Our understanding and practice of Inclusivity is the principal way to meet our challenges in the 21st Century.

2.3 Advocacy of the Whole

We have all become adept at the "advocacy of the parts." We see our own special interest group so narrowly that we automatically exclude all who are contrary to our position. Politicians get elected on the strength of how different they are from the other groups, not how much we are alike. The "Advocacy of the Parts" has become so stratified that it is difficult to see who actually holds a common vision for a community, culture or country.

We have lost our sense of community, not just in relatively isolated areas like small towns but throughout the developed world. We have lost our larger sense of the whole, of what "our country" means. We have lost a shared sense of destiny. We have lost a common vision.

Saying we lost our vision may not be accurate: we may never have had a sense of community that included everyone. Our country's past is littered with ethnic strife, class divisions and social conflict.

Now is the time to develop a common vision, not just for the country but also for the whole world. Now is the time to develop the authentic, committed, compassionate participants in that vision. That is the purpose of this course.

2.4 The Opportunity: Conscious Evolution

We now have an opportunity that never before existed in human history: the technology to create the world's first global human society. If we are to transform our world, we must reach out to every segment of our society with the philosophy of inclusivity. Let's explore how we really embrace that as a goal.

How do we sit down with our Other and say, "Let's talk?" Are we too busy trying to make them wrong? Are we so single-minded that we refuse to associate with those who disagree with us? Are we willing to find out that we are not so different from "the Other" after all? Do we rely on "enemy thinking" to create our own identity?

LEARNING DISCUSSION OF CHAPTER TWO

Consult your journal before answering these questions:

For Each Section:

- What was one thing you agreed with?

- What was one thing you didn't understand, or you disagreed with?

For Each Exercise:

- What was your experience of the exercise?

- What did you learn? What will you take away?

- What did you find unclear or difficult?

For the Chapter:

- What was your strongest take-away from this chapter?

- What was your most difficult or challenging concept to practice?

- What was the most interesting thing you wrote after your meditation?

> ### MEDITATION
> Reflections on Your Personal Journey
> Conclude this chapter with a five- to ten-minute
> meditation. Record your reflections in your
> journal or below.

NOTES

Outcomes:

- To understand how the *Philosophy of Inclusivity* applies to oneself.

- To understand and recognize the forms of inter-personal disconnection.

- How to use meditation and other consciousness management tools to create and enhance inclusivity within oneself.

A human being is part of the whole, called by us "universe," a part limited in time and space. He experiences himself, his thoughts and feelings, as something separated from the rest— a kind of delusion of his consciousness. This delusion is a prison for us, restricting us to our personal desires and to affection for a few persons nearest to us. Our task must be to free ourselves from this prison by widening our circle of compassion to embrace all living creatures and the whole of nature in its beauty.

—Albert Einstein

(quoted in Creating a World That Works for All)

MEDITATION
Start with a 5-10 minute meditation.
Record your beginning attitudes
and initial impressions in your journal.

A human being is part of the whole, called by us "universe," a part limited in time and space. He experiences himself, his thoughts and feelings, as something separated from the rest— a kind of delusion of his consciousness. This delusion is a prison for us, restricting us to our personal desires and to affection for a few persons nearest to us. Our task must be to free ourselves from this prison by widening our circle of compassion to embrace all living creatures and the whole of nature in its beauty.

—Albert Einstein
(quoted in *Creating a World That Works for All*)

3.1 Overview: Connection and Disconnection within the Self

In modern society, we experience a fundamental disconnect. We feel disconnected from each other, disconnected from nature, even disconnected from ourselves. This is what Einstein referred to as the "delusion of consciousness." (I would call it "the delusion of individuality and exclusivity.") And, unfortunately, it is reinforced almost every second of every day by Breaker society.

In Keeper cultures (cultures having roots in their indigenous experience), children are raised believing that they are connected to the whole, to all other beings. They are raised to have a strong connection and reverence for their:

- **Tribe** including ancestors, elders, wisdom-teachers and healers.

- **Community** including family members and the young.

- **Environment** including food, natural resources and nature's cycles.

- **Other beings** including other species and spiritual guides.

In modern society, these relationships are broken:
- Tribe doesn't exist.

- Community is either conceptual or meaningless.

- Environment is transformed for convenience, or ignored.

- Food comes packaged and divorced from its living connections (most children in the US have no idea where milk comes from).

- Other beings are either ignored or treated with fear, contempt and suspicion (or turned into pets).

- Ancestors are unknown.

3.2 Connection and Disconnection within the Self: Internal Exclusivity and the Delusion of Separation

We experienced internal exclusivity, starting from a very young age, as we developed our sense of Self as being different from others. WE were TAUGHT this difference. We were taught to compare ourselves with others. People acted toward us as though we were separate. We notice others' actions, possessions, popularity, power and the many other trappings of success of those around us.

From this process, we develop an external view of our own lives. We are taught to make value judgments about these externalities. We are taught that these external factors make us "good" or "bad," "successful" or "failures." We begin to think that we <u>are</u> our cars, jobs, homes and other physical possessions and attributes.

It doesn't stop with our physical possessions: Having the right degree, club membership, spouse, body or religion.

This, of course, is delusion. A car is a device that transports us; spending $100,000 for a car does not get you to your destination faster. A watch is a device that tells time; spending $50,000 for a watch does not give you more time, or a higher quality of time. These things cannot tell us who we are, cannot give us a sense of ourselves, cannot give meaning or value to our lives.

However, just because it is a delusion does not mean it cannot rule us, cannot be the focus of our pain and suffering. The car or the watch or the club membership does not cause suffering; not knowing who we are and covering it up by coveting these external devices causes the pain and suffering.

Many of us don't try to wake up from our delusions—we love our delusions, and will fight to maintain them. We just don't want them to hurt. But, often they do hurt, so we even delude ourselves about the effects of our delusions.

Many of us seek ways to relieve the resulting pain we feel from maintaining our delusions. Some use psychotherapy. We don't want to <u>end</u> the delusion ... we just want it to make us <u>happy</u>. That's a situation where the blind are leading the blind—we try to free ourselves from delusion by seeking help from people who are delusional themselves. We are learning that merely swapping delusions does not work. [1]

Others attempt to be free of pain through either overstimulation or deadening of the senses. Alcohol, recreational drugs, stimulating "entertainment" and television are common "pain relievers." In its extremes, we may use suicide or homicide as ways to rid ourselves of the pain caused by our delusions.

In fact, we will do almost anything—except actually wake up from the delusions themselves.

---

[1] I am not implying that all psychotherapy is delusional. There are many individuals who are helped by it. However, as a society, psychotherapy in the US is helping us connect to our dysfunctional "norm." For more on this, see psychologist James Hillman's book, *We've Had a Hundred Years of Psychotherapy — And the World's Getting Worse*.

3.2.1 The Experience of Internal Exclusivity

At its extremes, the internal exclusivity that Einstein refers to as "a delusion of consciousness" manifests as schizophrenia, bipolar disorders, anorexia, alcoholism, obsessive-compulsive disorder and other debilitating mental/emotional conditions. However, most of us experience milder forms of internal exclusivity, that manifest as some level of inner conflict, confusion or dysfunction.

The purpose of this section is not to "cure" anyone. The purpose is to become AWARE of our internal conflicts in our bodies, our minds, our emotions and even the experience of our spirits. If we can become aware of these internal conflicts, we can understand and manage them. Once we see how internal exclusivity manifests itself in our lives, we can take action to stop it within ourselves and recognize when others are being driven by it.

Our purpose is not to manage our delusions of separation and exclusivity. Our purpose is to wake up.

3.2.2 Bodily (Physical) Inclusivity

Internal exclusivity can be defined as being separate from parts/aspects of oneself — that what I do to/with one aspect of "me" has no effect on any other aspect. Bodily exclusivity is being separated from various aspects and functions of one's body, one's self.

How many of us behave in ways that we know are not good for us? From drinking coffee to taking heroin, from smoking cigarettes to not exercising, from eating junk food to binge drinking.

Our separation from our bodies may be more subtle, like a person who doesn't feel they are thin enough to be considered beautiful, muscular enough to be considered desirable or have the right skin color to be accepted.

Our separation from our own bodies causes both physical and emotional pain and suffering. We may feel inferior to others, because we don't have THEIR body (wrong size, color, conditions). Suicide may be the ultimate form of bodily exclusivity.

However, not every experience of bodily pain and suffering is the result of exclusivity from oneself. Elite athletes, for example, train to push themselves past psychological limits to achieve excellence in their sports. A person goes to the dentist and endures discomfort and pain, in order to avoid deeper pain later on.

Bodily inclusivity means that we have recognized that we are inextricably linked to our bodies. This means that we are aware of and accept all aspects of our bodies as aspects of ourselves, that our depth of being includes our bodies.

Bodily inclusivity means having a positive self-image regarding our bodies.

EXERCISE: **Inventory of Your Body**

1. List the things that you currently do to/for your body that are good/positive for the long-term health of your body. (Include exercise, eating good, healthy food, meditating and creative activities.)

2. List the things that you currently do to/for your body that are bad/negative for the long-term health of your body. (Include over-eating, eating bad food, ingesting toxic substances, etc.)

3. List the good/positive things that you SHOULD/WOULD LIKE TO do to/for your body that you currently don't.

4. List the bad/negative things that you SHOULD NOT/WOULD LIKE NOT TO do to/for your body that you currently do.

Review your lists and decide on five activities that you want to continue or start to incorporate into your daily behavior to increase your bodily inclusivity.

3.2.3 Mental Exclusivity

Many of us feel a sense of separation from our minds. Mental exclusivity is being separate from parts of one's own mind or thoughts.

We talk about "my ego" or "my id" or "my personality" or "my depression" as though they are items that sit on a shelf waiting for us to take them down and wear them. As though they are separate from self. In its extreme, mental exclusivity shows up as schizophrenia, bipolar, etc. Also, extreme drug-taking and alcoholism may be examples of ultimate mental exclusivity.

In lesser examples, it is the constant internal critic/judge that judges one's own thoughts, actions and beliefs as "bad." Some self-criticism is necessary and good. (You just finished a critical self-assessment in the prior chapter!) When the critic/judge prevents you from being functional in the world, that is a form of mental exclusivity.

A person may decide to change something about themselves. They can do so as a judging critic ("I'm bad"). Or, they can do so through acceptance and connection. ("I am X and I choose to change to Y.")

We act as though our minds are separate from self. We treat our minds with chemicals so that we will not feel depressed. We want our thoughts and feelings to fall in line with everyone else's thoughts and feelings so we follow the social trends and norms. We force our personalities to fall into socially acceptable norms. We feed our minds a steady diet of television, the junk food of the brain.

Our lack of mental inclusivity can negatively affect our ability to function in the world. In extreme cases, people punish and/or mutilate themselves, experience anorexia and bulimia, and become violent with self.

3.2.4 Mental Inclusivity

Practicing inclusivity of the mind and personality means that we recognize that we are not separate from our mental processes, and that we can bring our mental processes into Oneness.

Just as we have had experiences of mental exclusivity, we also have glimpses of inclusivity within the mental realm. One example would be the spontaneous experiences where your thoughts melt away, and you find yourself in a quiet and profoundly deep state of mind. This reduction of what is sometimes referred to as "monkey mind", happens when one is experiencing a state of peace.

You do not have to wait for this to happen spontaneously. You can work to make this mental state occur. This is called "meditation." By meditation, I mean one of any number of techniques to:
- Still and quiet the mind

- Reduce sensory input

- Concentrate and focus the attention

- Connect with nonlocal and Transcendent energy.

Under the general topic of meditation, these techniques include:
- Sitting in silent awareness

- Walking

- Chanting

- Singing
-
- Ritual movement

- Breath control

- Sensory deprivation

- Contemplation on a ritual object

- Many, many other techniques.

In this regard, we can think of meditation as "personal consciousness management." All of us recognize the benefits of regular physical exercise (personal physical management) even when we don't get it. Many people do mental exercises, like solving crossword puzzles, to keep the mental faculties sharp. Meditation is just like that — building coherence between our hearts and minds, and increasing the likelihood of connecting our hearts and minds with others.

One important point regarding meditation: it simply does not matter what religious or spiritual tradition is used for the meditation. Many people will claim that one technique is superior to another, or will claim that only their own technique "works." However, the work of Dr. Larry Dossey and others prove that any and all types of prayer and meditation, practiced with sincerity, are equally effective.

If you do not manage your consciousness, who will? Remember: there are literally MILLIONS of people, earning BILLIONS of dollars, who want to "manage" you into buying their products and services. They want to tell you what to think, how to react, and what to buy.

Manage yourself ...

3.2.5 Emotional Exclusivity

Emotional exclusivity is feeling separate from aspects of our emotional state, or feeling no emotions at all — numbing.

Teenage mutilation — scarring one's arms and legs with a razor blade, for example, is becoming increasingly common. This behavior is an example of emotional exclusivity — doing something that causes pain and suffering to oneself. (It is also an example of "bodily exclusivity," the hand causing injury to the arm.) A person experiencing emotional exclusivity may do an action that causes discomfort or pain (for example, in relationships, work or even physical exercise), but may be so disconnected from their emotions that they are not consciously aware of their discomforts.

People experiencing emotional exclusivity are separated from their own sources of emotional joy and happiness — they do the opposite of that which would make them happy. The ultimate expression of emotional exclusivity is suicide, which is at an all-time high in our society.

Of course, not all self-inflicted emotional pain represents emotional exclusivity. We consciously take on pain and suffering, if we believe that it will help us to become a better person in the long run. Or, we may choose to share the emotional burden of another, in an attempt to lighten their load. (For example,

we may choose to grieve with a friend or loved one, to help lighten their emotional burden.) In fact, this ability to take on conscious suffering and/or delay gratification is one of the things that makes us human.

We will also take pain and suffering onto ourselves, for the sake of another. For example, the parent who takes on pain for their children's benefit or the rescuer who runs into a burning building to rescue others.

Finally, there are those who take on pain, suffering and discomfort for spiritual development and growth. Forms of this may include fasting, extreme yoga postures, and ritual prostrations.

In each of these examples, the person experiencing the pain or discomfort intends to do so for a higher purpose. This is the opposite of those experiencing emotional exclusivity, who take on pain and suffering for no reason, or for reasons that are not elevating, but debilitating and depressing.

One only has to look at the statistics for suicide and depression in our society to see the prevalence of emotional exclusivity. Less extreme but perhaps more numerous are those people who think negative thoughts about themselves, who "hate" themselves (or some aspect of themselves).

3.2.6 Emotional Inclusivity

People who practice emotional inclusivity are emotionally integrated. They experience a full range of emotional expression, from joy and ecstasy to doubt and depression — without bogging down in any emotional state.

Emotional inclusivity does not mean "happy all the time." A person who experiences nothing but happy all the time is numb to the full range of human emotions — and probably isn't paying attention to the world around them. (Or, perhaps they have achieved a state or level of spiritual mastery. I have not encountered any people who fit this category.)

Emotions — both positive and negative — are experienced and appropriately expressed, but the emotionally whole personality does not IDENTIFY with any emotional state.

A person experiencing emotional inclusivity understands that the background condition of the Universe is Love. (This universal Love is not the emotional experience of "love" as a desire state between humans, but Love as a foundational state for All That Is.) As such, negative emotional states are experienced as only conditional, temporary and non-permanent.

3.2.7 Spiritual Exclusivity

One of the most fundamental disconnects in our society is the separation people experience between themselves and their own spirit, between themselves and Transcendent Reality—the world beyond the five senses.

By spiritual experience, we are NOT talking about religious experiences. Many religious experiences are spiritual, but many are not. And, many spiritual experiences have nothing to do with religious practices. There are many access points to the Transcendent. Religion has been one for many people, but there are many, many others.

We have a deep need for transpersonal, transcendent connection. Many of us have lost the ability to achieve it. This disconnect is called "spiritual starvation," not knowing how to get fed. [2] Spiritual starvation is the spiritual disconnect that feeds and fuels all of the others.

In Breaker societies, the world of inclusive Spirit is ignored and ridiculed, at the expense of our souls. We have built a tradition around rugged individualism, ignoring our real needs for caring, sharing, community and Transcendence.

Worse yet, in the light of not knowing how to get spiritually fed, many people in our culture have developed an entire philosophy that says it is UNIMPORTANT to have connection with the Transcendent, the Divine. That either there is no Divine, or that the Divine is not as important as Man is. "I am separate from the Divine" is the ultimate in "I am separate" thinking.

The lack of awareness of our spiritual connections leads to a delusion that is called the "God Complex," the delusion that one believes that humans are the most important (or only) divinity in the Universe. [3] This is one of the bulwarks of the Breaker philosophy (also known as "Modernity").

In this thinking, our "spiritual" lives are relegated to a set of cultural behaviors and rituals practiced a few hours, one day a week. These practices may be cultural, in that they represent shared behavior, but may not be spiritual, in that the behavior does not lead to Transcendence. This leads to confusion between spirituality and culture; we begin to mistake certain cultural practices as spiritual practices. We do this because we cannot feel the difference.

Outside of a few hours on the weekend and perhaps some religious holidays, many of us act as though HUMANS were the most important beings in the Universe.

---

[2] Refer to Chapter 2 of *Creating a World That Works for All*
[3] See http://en.wikipedia.org/wiki/God_complex

3.2.8 Spiritual Inclusivity

We practice spiritual inclusivity in three directions: spiritual community with each other, Earth connections and spiritual transcendence.

Community: It is in community that we have our first experience of the Transcendent, of an experience larger than our individual selves. Many of us have had the experience of a group activity that takes us outside of our bodily selves. This may be a group meditation or a basketball game. Whatever the trigger, we suddenly feel as though we are an integral part of the experience. We are LARGER, more CONNECTED and more INTEGRATED than before. It may feel like a mystical experience—a shared experience that cannot be expressed in words (yes, even in a basketball game).

Earth: Our experience of the Transcendent may come from a more-than-human experience, an encounter with the natural world. This may come from walking in the forest, seeing a sunset or looking into the eyes of a wild animal. In this experience we awaken, even if for a moment, to the awareness that there is another or additional reality other than that of our experience. We begin to see that there are other points of view, beyond the human. This can lead to the experience of pure bliss that is beyond all of our human experiences.

Transcendence: Unlike the prior examples, spiritual transcendence comes from an experience of reality that is larger than our senses, larger than the material world. Community and Earth transcendence takes place within the material world. Spiritual transcendence takes place beyond it.

"Beyond the senses" does not necessarily involve Ouija boards or séances. In the exercises below, you will experience a number of fairly common occurrences, each happening "beyond the senses." Spiritual transcendence also includes communicating with the "more than human" world. [4] In almost every Keeper tradition, there are stories of how human beings converse with other beings—especially ancestors and the beings that make up one's food supply.

Spiritual transcendence also covers those areas that have been traditionally the purview of the various religious traditions — communicating with, and receiving guidance from, beings who are beyond earthly existence. This may include communing with spirits, avatars, gods, goddesses, astral beings, ascended masters, etc. Even if one chooses not to believe in this particular level of transcendence, it does not negate the reality of the other forms of transcendence.

While there are many techniques that claim to induce or trigger a transcendental state or moment, ultimately, the experience of the transcendent is an act of grace. It is experienced when one sincerely opens to it.

From a world in which the Spirit has been systemically ignored, from a "dispirited" world, inclusivity means consciously recognizing a spirit in the world. Thomas Moore and others have called this the re-enchantment of the world. [5] According to Moore, re-enchantment means the return of beauty, imagination, harmony, mystery and a sense of the symbolic and poetic to the natural and manufactured world.

This re-enchantment comes from the very process of bringing people together past the barriers that separate them. Although the work is hard, the benefits are both practical and mystical. The practice of inclusivity helps people arrive at a higher level of community and approach the mystical oneness of the Divine.

EXERCISE: **Experiencing Transcendence**

Reflect on the questions below. Record your thoughts and feelings in your journal. Share the questions and your reflections with your practice friend. Discuss how you will use your insights in the future.

1. Have you ever felt someone staring at you? I call this "spider-sense." What are the circumstances where this feeling is more pronounced for you? For me, it is being in a foreign country, where I look very different from the norm, AND there are no cultural taboos *against staring at someone.* (For more on this, see Sheldrake, Rupert *The Sense of Being Stared At.*)

2. Have you been to a concert and heard a misplayed, bad note? Or, have you looked at a grouping of colors and seen that one of them is out of balance, the wrong shade? I call this harmony-sense. It is not just hearing or seeing—it is being able to tell when something is out of balance.

3. Can you, without looking at a clock, tell how much time has passed? Or have an accurate sense of the time, without looking at a clock? Or, regularly wake up a few minutes before your alarm goes off—regardless of what time you set it for? I call this time-sense.

4. Have you witnessed dogs who know when their masters are coming home? Have you had a psychic relationship with animals? (For more on this, see Sheldrake, Rupert *Dogs that Know When Their Owners Are Coming Home.*)

5. What other experiences do you have of transcendent senses?

---

[4] See : *In the Spirit of the Earth* by Calvin Luther Martin.
[5] Moore, Thomas, *The Re-Enchantment of Everyday Life*

3 .3 Internal Inclusivity ... and Leadership

What happens when a person who experiences internal exclusivity takes on a leadership position? For them, leadership is defined by what they personally receive from the experience. Generally, they tend to support the largest group to which they identify, and oppose the most different group they can find. In the case of Adolph Hitler, this meant supporting blond-haired German Aryans (although he was a dark-haired Austrian) and opposing Jews (although a Jewish doctor saved his life in WWI and he had no personal negative experiences with them).

This form of leadership has been very effective in the world: talk up the good guys, talk down the bad guys, and let everybody take sides. It's what's gotten the world into the shape it is in today. Exclusivist leadership is one of the things in our society that has to <u>change</u> .

Although we have fewer examples, there are instances of people who have a high degree of internal inclusivity assuming leadership positions. In modern times, these examples would include Mahatma Gandhi, Martin Luther King, Vaclav Havel and Aung San Suu Kyi.

A common factor among the above leaders is that people see them as "spiritual" — despite the fact that they represented very different religious traditions (Hindu, Christian and Buddhist) and their work was very secular, rooted in current political realities. I believe that this spiritual leadership comes from:

- Clear values.

- Universally held values.

- Personal behavior in alignment with values.

- Having goals, visions and objectives in alignment with personal values and needs of the larger society.

- Holding a vision of a society that includes all.

Living one's values, and doing so for the sake of others, elevates one's perspective.
This gives us an interesting perspective: the person in a leadership position with a high degree of internal inclusivity is seen as a spiritual leader. It's not just that they have spiritual knowledge — most of us have that. It's that their values form the foundation of their lives and their work. Being motivated by what we cannot perceive — by what lies beyond the senses — this makes us spiritual leaders

LEARNING DISCUSSION OF CHAPTER THREE

Consult your journal before answering these questions:

For Each Section:

- What was one thing you agreed with?

- What was one thing you didn't understand, or you disagreed with?

For Each Exercise:

- What was your experience of the exercise?

- What did you learn? What will you take away?

- What did you find unclear or difficult?

For the Chapter:

- What was your strongest take-away from this chapter?

- What was your most difficult or challenging concept to practice?

- What was the most interesting thing you wrote after your meditation?

> MEDITATION
> Reflections on Your Personal Journey
> Conclude this chapter with a five- to ten-minute
> meditation. Record your reflections in your
> journal or below.

NOTES

Outcomes:

- To understand how to embrace cultural change without fear.

- To identify internal filters.

- To understand how to practice the twelve steps of including the Other.

- To effectively address and resolve deep-rooted, systemic differences.

- To know the steps of building inclusive community.

"If your vision is for a year, plant wheat.
If your vision is for ten years, plant trees.
If your vision is for a lifetime, plant people."
—Chinese Proverb

MEDITATION
Start with a 5-10 minute meditation.
Record your beginning attitudes
and initial impressions in your journal.

"If your vision is for a year, plant wheat.
If your vision is for ten years, plant trees.
If your vision is for a lifetime, plant people."
—Chinese Proverb

4.1 Overview: The Experience of Inclusivity with Others

We live in a society where we routinely practice exclusivity, the belief that we are separate from other people. This illusion of separation exists and is reinforced in all aspects of life. Exclusivity manifests itself in various ways, including racism, sexism, homophobia, and a disrespect for the natural world.

To heal our society and our planet, we must learn to practice social inclusivity, practicing the belief that we are inextricably linked to one another. Inclusivity is not dependent on whether or not we like each other, or whether or not we tolerate each other. Inclusivity is not a preference but a way of experiencing reality. Inclusivity work goes far beyond traditional diversity training:

- Traditional diversity training will look at two or three legally protected classes.
- With inclusivity, we examine many (20+) factors that influence human behavior, including culture, class, history, ideology … All together, we call these factors "dēmos-dynamics," the dynamic interactions of groups of people.

- The methodology of diversity training is to help us see and appreciate our differences. The methodology of inclusivity training is to help us see how we are alike in our reactions to the Other.

- The purpose of diversity training is to get us to like, appreciate, or tolerate people within certain legally protected classes. The purpose of inclusivity training is to get us to recognize that we are One, that we are the Other to someone else, and that our challenges extend beyond the legally protected classes.

4.2 Who Is the Other?

Who is the Other? Simply, the Other is the person or group with whom you find it hardest to practice inclusivity, the group from whom you feel the most separation. The Other may be a person of a different ethnicity, class, religion, and/or ideology. The Other may be a parent or a spouse.

All of us have someone who is, for us, the Other. All of us experience degrees of separation from other people. The challenge of the 21st Century is not to act on our feelings of separation. Our challenge is to act like we are all brothers and sisters, not strangers and enemies. [6]

If we are to transform our world, we must reach out to every segment of our society. **We have to reach out to the Other.** That sounds like a worthwhile goal. However, how do we <u>really</u> reach out to those who are of a different class, a different ethnicity, a different culture, a different religion, or a different ideology?

How do we reach out to those who act, speak or think in ways that are different, even foreign, to our own? How do we reach out to those who are hostile, resistant, defended, in pain?

It's easy to avoid the Other in a society that makes connecting difficult. It is relatively easy for us to put ourselves in a bubble of sameness, then convince ourselves that our bubble is the world.

What do we do when the Other is in the same group (organization, family region), and professes to share the same goals?

---

[6] Adapted from a chapter written by Sharif Abdullah entitled "The Soul of a Terrorist," published in *The Psychology of Terrorism* Chris Stout, ed.

EXERCISE: **The Inclusivity Quotient Test**

This test will help you see the degree of inclusivity in your associations with others. There is no right or wrong answer; high or low score. The In-Q Test just shows your patterning. To download the test: go to www.commonway.org/node/217.

To take the test, just rate each category or group along the five columns on the test sheet (see handout). Don't spend a lot of time thinking about or analyzing your choices. Give your first, gut reactions, not what you think is the politically correct response.

On the form: Place a check mark in the appropriate column:

1.   Our People: People you most identify with. If you are a bicyclist, you would rate other bicyclists as our people.

2.   My Friends: People you do not identify with, but have positive, pleasant associations.

3.   Neutral/No Opinion: People you don't know about, or have formed no particular opinion about.

4.   Those People: People who have a negative association for you. A general sense of un- ease, dislike or you would rather not be around.

5.   The Enemy: People for whom you have a strong negative reaction. People you definitely do not want to be around or associate with.

Don't try to be politically correct, or give answers based on what you think others would say or what would be popular — just give your honest answers.

Scoring: Add each column. Then, add across the columns for a total In-Q score.

DISCUSSION: Share and discuss a few of your responses with your discussion group. Choose three of your "Our People" choices and three of your "The Enemy" choices.

What the Scores Mean

1.   Are most of your scores bunched around the neutral column? Not having strong feelings may indicate a calm personality, but may also indicate a lack of honest interaction with others in the world.

2.   Are most of your scores bunched in the positive columns? This may indicate a person who gets along well with others, but it may also indicate that you were giving politically correct answers — ones that may be in variance with your true feelings.

3.   Are most of your scores bunched in the negative columns? This may indicate strongly held feelings about trusting others. Where did these opinions originate? How can you change them?

A high score of 165 means you have a perfect *In-Q* Score. It also means that you aren't being particularly honest about taking the test! The same goes for a perfect negative score of (–)165.

EXERCISE: **Seeing the Other**

1. Where do you experience boundaries (race, class, ideology)?

2. For you, who is the Other?

3. What causes you to separate from the Other?

4. Where/when/how do you transcend those boundaries?

5. What would it take for you to overcome the illusion of separation?

6. What are your experiences with the Other (positive and negative)?

7. How do we interact with the Other?

8. What creates the CONTEXT for dealing with the Other?

4.3 Dealing with Our Otherness: the Challenge of a Global Society

For most of our time on this planet, up until a few decades ago, the vast majority of people did not have to deal with the Other. People were born, raised, educated, worked, married, lived and died in the same neighborhood. Even within multi-ethnic cities, a person rarely traveled to another quarter, and when they did, interactions were limited and controlled.

Most governments are simply the codification and enforcement of culture. Examples of this include state-enforced segregation, the criminalization of marijuana use (but not alcohol use), laws against polygamy, etc.

In the past, interactions were controlled by the dominant culture. You were asked to conform to the dominant culture, unless you are in a specific cultural quarter, and then you were expected to conform to the culture of that quarter.

Now, most of us interact in a world where we have regular contact with people who are Other.

4.4 Identifying the Types of Otherness

1. Physical
- Race/Ethnicity
- Gender
- Physical Attributes (height, hair, eyes, skin)
- Physical Ability

2. Behavioral .
- Language
- Culture
- Mental/Emotional
- Sexual Orientation

3. Ideological
- Religion
- Political/National Origin
- Perspectives/Points of View

Combinations
- Poor Whites: Race/Culture/Class Issues
- Irish Americans: Politics/Ethnicity/Faith/Class Issues
- Amish/Pennsylvania Dutch: Culture/Language/Class/Religious Issues
- Israelis/Palestinians: Ethnicity/Culture/Language/Class/Religious Issues

---

4.5 Addressing Otherness

It is difficult for us to hear those who are "different."

4.5.1 Fear of the Other: The Opposite of Inclusivity

Why are we so afraid of the Other? Why do we tend to avoid those who are different?

This has to do with the nature of consciousness. Most of our behaviors are performed automatically—even complex behaviors like cooking or driving a car.

Our conscious minds kick in when we are confronted with something that does not have an automated response—when we face the new. We use our consciousness for that which we are unsure of. And that uncertainty has a level of apprehension or threat attached. If things were not scary, you would have an automated response already.

4.5.2 Prejudice, Bigotry and Hate Crimes

Sometimes, we use differences between people as a way to build community with the group. From an unkind remark to racist or religious violence, each act is designed to build support for Group A by tearing down Group B. Many people who would never make a racist statement have no problem ridiculing someone based on class or ideology. It's all social exclusivity.

4.5.3 Protocols and Political Correctness

In the face of being insecure about the Other, we create rules of conduct that place on each group's behavior an acceptable norm. Political correctness encourages us to use certain words and behaviors in order to prevent injury to the Other—even when it does. And, political correctness prevents and avoids words and behaviors that cause injury to the Other— even when it doesn't. Political correctness is used as a code to impute intentions — if you say the correct words, we will impute positive intentions to you. or your or ideology. It's all social exclusivity.

4.6 Overcoming Otherness, Transcending Difference

We ERASE our differences with the Other when there is an overriding common goal.
- People will do intense, intimate, interpersonal sharing with total strangers, given the proper context (for example, the group sharing sessions of Al-Anon and other 12-Step programs).

- In the face of earthquakes and other widespread disasters, people will ignore barriers of race, class and other separators.

- People will risk their lives to save others, many times total strangers.

We erase our differences with the Other when there is an overriding cultural mandate to do so.
- Military

- Work

- School

EXERCISE: **Transcending Difference**

1. When have you experienced an overriding common goal?

2. What was the effect (if any) on how you experienced culture?

3. What cultural circumstances have weakened barriers to the Other for you?

Inclusive Action #1:
Redefining the Other: Seeking the Larger Whole

What is the largest group to which you identify? For some, that will be their culture, nationality or gender. We are aiming for still larger ways of defining Us. Ultimately, all human beings form one family.

Inclusive Action #2:
Celebrate Difference — Practice Diversity

1. Are you conscious about practicing inclusivity in all aspects of your life?

2. Which forms of inclusivity are easy for you? Which ones harder?

3. Do you regularly interact with people who hold widely divergent viewpoints from yours?

    a. How do you feel about these interactions?

    b. Do you think the interactions are valuable?

    c. Are you aware of trying to change their viewpoint to yours? Vice versa?

    d. How do you feel about that?

4. How do others view you when you are interacting with people who are different?

Inclusive Action #3:
Celebrate Oneness — Practice Inclusivity

1. Do you try to foster inclusivity? What steps do you take to include the Other in your activities?
    - Personal

    - Social

    - Organizational

2. What are some of the challenges to creating truly inclusive activities?

3. Have you gone onto the "home base" of your Other in order to interact with them on their terms? What was the result?

4. Will you go onto the "home base" of your Other in order to interact with them on their terms? Why? Why not?

Inclusive Action #4:
Perceiving Commonalities —
Stop Thinking that You (or Them) Are Separate or Different

Exclusivity comes when you believe that you are different. (It is true that all of us are "different." We are each distinct humans. However, it is truer that we are connected.) What are some of the techniques you utilize to overcome the illusion of being separate or different?

Inclusive Action #5:
Get Direct with People

1. What percentage of your significant human connection is through an intervening technology (telephone, email, Internet)?

2. What percentage is face-to-face?

Inclusive Action #6:
Walking Past Fear — Stop Letting Fear Dictate Your Actions

1. What fears or uncertainties did you hold in the past regarding a former Other?

2. What fears or uncertainties do you now hold regarding a current Other?

EXERCISE: **12 STEPS IN PRACTICING ENGAGEMENT**

1. Acknowledge the Other as a part of the whole/divine.

2. Help the Other to calm themselves before trying to communicate. Try to encourage them to be excited but not agitated. (Research shows that people stop reasoning when agitated, angry or fearful. When a person's heart rate is 125 beats per minute or above, the reasoning part of the brain shuts down and the fight-or-flight response takes over. See *Blink* by Malcom Gladwell.)

3. Listen to the Other's position. Practice active listening.

4. *Rest*ate the Other's position to him/her. Re-word, remove or transform politically, ethnically or culturally charged separatist language.

5. Acknowledge the validity of his or her position (or, at least the parts of it that you think are valid). As much as possible, incorporate the Other's position into your own. This becomes your new negotiating position. (This means that the Other will change you in some profound ways. Let that happen. It's the only way that you will be able to change the Other in profound ways.)

6. Acknowledge the validity of the feelings and fears that drove the Other to his or her contending position. Be compassionate. Practice place transference; put yourself in the Other's place. Acknowledge the feelings—feelings are always valid (even if the facts driving the feelings are not).

7. State your own intentions and goals. Include the parts you incorporated from the Other's position. State your goals in a positive, powerful, unequivocal way.

8. State your core values, which should include inclusivity, nonviolence, mutual respect and spiritual power.

9. State your core fears. Be honest.

10. Invite the Other to state their core values. (Very important: help the Other see the difference between core values and core fears.) Invite the Other to separate the parts of their position that are core values.

11. Invite the Other to your goal (especially since it now incorporates parts of their goals.)

12. If they decline, invite the Other to re-state their position in a way that includes all sides. Patiently work with them to do the restatement. Continue to do the restatement of positions and values until the core issues are resolved.

LEARNING DISCUSSION OF CHAPTER FOUR

Consult your journal before answering these questions:

For Each Section:

- What was one thing you agreed with?

- What was one thing you didn't understand, or you disagreed with?

For Each Exercise:

- What was your experience of the exercise?

- What did you learn? What will you take away?

- What did you find unclear or difficult?

For the Chapter:

- What was your strongest take-away from this chapter?

- What was your most difficult or challenging concept to practice?

- What was the most interesting thing you wrote after your meditation?

> ## MEDITATION
> Reflections on Your Personal Journey
> Conclude this chapter with a five- to ten-minute
> meditation. Record your reflections in your
> journal or below.

Outcomes:

- To understand the difference between inclusivity and exclusivity in a societal (political) context.

- To understand the models, tools and perceived benefits of exclusivist social/political action.

- To understand the models, tools and perceived benefits of inclusivist social/political action.

"The secret is to gang up on the problem, rather than each other."

—Thomas Stallkamp

MEDITATION
Start with a 5-10 minute meditation.
Record your beginning attitudes
and initial impressions in your journal.

*"The secret is to gang up on the problem,
rather than each other."*

—Thomas Stallkamp

5.1 Overview: The Experience of Inclusivity in Society

Inclusivity and politics are intertwined. (By politics, we mean how we govern each other's behavior.)

Societal exclusivity is defined as how we govern behavior for the benefit of me and my group.

We can see that this is the dominant form of political discourse, in our society and in the world at this time. While individuals and groups claim to represent the interests of the whole, most do not even try.

In a practical sense, societal inclusivity is defined as how we govern behavior for the benefit of ALL. This means developing ways to identify, enhance and share power, collaborate between groups and resolve conflicts.

5.1.1 Social Capital

Social capital is a term that has received increasing attention from scholars and community activists. It is defined as social organization that, in the words of Robert Putnam, "facilitates coordination and cooperation for mutual benefit." In short, it is the willingness of people to do good things for other people—in other words, community.

Social capital is built over time; those systems with a high tradition of social interaction have higher social capital. Social capital has a number of characteristics:
1. Mutual confidence

2. Security

3. Trust

4. Organized reciprocity

5. Built over time (traditions, cultures)

6. Good reputation

7. Shared perspectives

Social capital is built when people come together to achieve a common purpose or activity whether it is an Amish barn raising, a soup kitchen in a church or a neighborhood watch group.

Social capital is built even when the common purpose or activity itself has nothing to do with creating a better civic life or building community trust. The activity does not have to intend to create social capital; it does so by virtue of the nature of the experience. Therefore, social capital can be built through organizations like:
• Networks

• Clubs

• Civic associations

• Religious groups

• Activist demonstrations

Even an entire city may have and strengthen social capital. In Portland, Oregon, for example, there is a common practice of road courtesy where drivers wait at intersections for pedestrians to pass or maneuver around minor traffic infractions without honking their horns.

EXERCISE: SOCIAL CAPITAL

- What experiences in building social capital do you have? Have you participated in a "barn raising" activity?

- Do you see yourself as the beneficiary of the social capital activities of others?

5.1.2 Exclusivity and Social Capital

Social capital is not the same as inclusivity. Social capital can be developed in ways that breed social and political **exclusivity**. Historically, the way some groups build social capital is at the expense of others. Infamous human organizations like the Nazi Party, Ku Klux Klan or the Mafia represent exclusivist social capital—developed at the expense of the Other—often living in the same community, for example, KKK members terrorizing citizens of their own community.

EXERCISE: **EXPERIENCES IN SOCIAL CAPITAL**

- What experiences do you have of negative social capital?

- What experiences do you have as a member of an excluding group?

- What was the impact (on you and/or others) of those experiences?

- What were the experiences you had as a member of an excluded group?

- What was the impact (on you and/or others) of those experiences?

5.2 Political Inclusivity and Empowerment

Political inclusivity means including all people in the power and decision-making structures and systems of a society, including historically excluded people. Empowerment takes place when all people involved and impacted by decisions are included in the decision-making processes. (All who want or desire to be involved.)

5.2.1 The Exclusivist Political Paradigm

Political exclusivity happens when decisions are made in isolation, removed from the people affected by the decisions.

Historically, this model was the way powerless people gained a share of power to change their communities. This was true when there were limited communications or institutions between groups of people. These tools enabled the powerless to:

- Organize quickly.

- Feel superior and better than (or, at least equal to) the Other.

- Work off their anger.

Because there was a perceived upside in the form of historical wins, like the Labor Movement and Civil Rights Movement, people continue to use this model, even though returns are now limited.

continue to use this model, even though returns are now limited.

Nowadays, political exclusivity breeds disempowerment, ignorance, suspicion, anger and apathy.

The exclusivist models include:
- Two party (or multi-party) governance structures.
- Us-versus-them social organizing (Acorn).
- Terrorism.

Exclusive political action includes behaviors that are very familiar to most of us:
- Strikes
- Boycotts
- Demonstrations
- Protests
- Polarizing (us-versus-them) political campaigns
- Violence

We also know how the exclusivist organizing tools work:
- Our group sets the agenda and determines what needs to be changed (in isolation from the Other).
- We align with (or oppose) whoever has power over the situation.
- We demonize the Other and make sure everyone understands what is wrong with them.
- We use whatever strategy is acceptable to our group to coerce the Other to comply including force, misinformation, intimidation and violence.
- We listen to the opposing side only to get ammunition to refute their position.

- We unite with people who agree with us to defeat the Other.
- We look for allies with everyone affected as we are by the issue on the agenda. "The enemy of my enemy is my friend."
- We create alliances: this means getting others to buy in to our agenda.
- Winning = realizing our agenda — at the expense of the Other.
- Winning = defeating the agenda of the Other.

What doesn't work about the exclusivist organizing model is that it:
- Generates fear. (The fear is long-lasting, much longer than the conflict itself. Many times, the generated fear goes on to fuel new conflicts.)
- Implies and supports us-versus-them (exclusivity and separatism, the keys of exclusivist politics).
- Diminishes inclusive social capital.
- Reinforces old power relationships.
- Can create unsatisfactory results — a win that is worse than the status quo.
- "Lesser of two evils" is evil.
- Existing power structure has built antibodies to exclusivist organizing models; exclusivist advocates must be responsible for the antibody reaction they produce.
- Low likelihood of lasting potential for change.
- Is increasingly difficult to find a "bad guy" around which to organize.

As we come to understand the complexity of "The Mess" (our inter-related mega-crises), we see that all of us to some extent are both victims and villains. No one is wholly at fault and no one is completely innocent.

EXERCISE: **YOUR EXPERIENCE WITH EXCLUSIVIST TOOLS**

As mentioned on page 51, exclusivist tools include:

- Strikes
- Boycotts
- Demonstrations
- Protests

- Polarizing (us-versus-them) political campaigns
- Violence

1. Have you used any of these tools before?

   a. When?

   b. Under what circumstances?

   c. What was the result?

   d. Did you achieve the goal?

   e. At what expense?

2. What are the circumstances where you think it is permissible/ acceptable to use these tools?

3. Can any of the exclusivist tools be applied as an inclusivist? Give examples.

5.2.2 The Inclusivist Political Paradigm

The inclusivity organizing model is taking shape due to the inadequacies of the declining paradigm of exclusivity.

The societal inclusivity organizing model:
- Inclusive of everyone.

- Builds social capital.

- Shares power.

- Doesn't reinforce old power relationships.

- Acknowledges cultural, social and religious differences without having them turn into barriers.

- Is empowering for all.

- Has higher potential for social change.

Societal inclusivity organizing tools:
- Non-agenda, visionary process: what is best for all parts of our community?

- Acknowledge that everyone has power in the situation.

- Acknowledge that power may be unevenly distributed.

- Building Community:
  * Unite with everyone (geographic reach and/or issue reach).

  * Unite with everyone affected, in any way, by the vision of your community.

  * Include those who are on all sides of the issue.

  * Build alliances across lines of separation BEFORE tackling issues.

  * Only use those tactics on others that you would want used with/on you.

  * Winning means realizing the vision in such a way that everyone buys in.

Those who are disaffected, reluctant, hostile or defended are the ones who create social conflict — or social capital.

LEARNING DISCUSSION OF CHAPTER FIVE

Consult your journal before answering these questions:

For Each Section:

- What was one thing you agreed with?

- What was one thing you didn't understand, or you disagreed with?

For Each Exercise:

- What was your experience of the exercise?

- What did you learn? What will you take away?

- What did you find unclear or difficult?

For the Chapter:

- What was your strongest take-away from this chapter?

- What was your most difficult or challenging concept to practice?

- What was the most interesting thing you wrote after your meditation?

> ## MEDITATION
> Reflections on Your Personal Journey
> Conclude this chapter with a five- to ten-minute
> meditation. Record your reflections in your
> journal or below.

SIX DEEP INCLUSIVITY: *THE INTERPLAY OF DEEP IDENTITY, DEEP CONFLICT AND DEEP CONNECTION*

Outcomes:

- To understand the core concepts of *Deep Identity, Deep Conflict* and *Deep Connection*.

- To correctly apply these concepts to ongoing conflict situations.

- To be able to step outside of one's own Deep Identity issues in order to assist others to resolve Deep Conflict issues.

- To understand the models, tools and perceived benefits of inclusivist social/political action.

"In Lak'ech."

**—A Maya greeting meaning
"I am another you."**

MEDITATION
Start with a 5-10 minute meditation.
Record your beginning attitudes
and initial impressions in your journal.

"In Lak'ech."

—**A Maya greeting meaning
"I am another you."**

6.**1 Overview: The Experience of Inclusivity in Society**

Much of the earlier sections of this course involve exclusivity or difference based on external issues — disputes over political ideologies or interpersonal relationships. In this section, we will focus on deep inclusivity, i.e., aspects of identity that are fundamental to one's sense of being. In this section, we will explore primary issues of inclusivity, and see how those primary issues may create intractable conflict. Our focus on deep inclusivity is one of the things that distinguishes this course from other forms of conflict resolution and/or facilitation.

Deep Inclusivity has [three] main aspects:

- Deep Identity

- Deep Conflict

- Deep Connection

6.2 What Is Deep Identity?

We have many different types of identity. We pick up some identities as we live our lives — spouse, student, jock, nerd, teacher, driver, celebrity, spouse, employee, owner or party member. These identities change, grow, evolve and end. They are not part of our foundational identities.

Some identities are given to us by our ancestry and are, therefore, stable, influential and unchangeable:
- Race and ethnicity

- Gender

- Family

Other aspects of our identities are given to us by our culture, and are, therefore, more mutable:
- Food

- Shelter

- Clothing

- Language

- Religion
-
- Relationship to Earth

Definition: Major aspects of our identity are given to us in our infancy. They are in place well BEFORE we develop the capacity to THINK about them. **Therefore, our Deep Identity is the part of our identity that we acquired before we acquired the capacity for rational thought.**

Child psychologists say that we humans are eight or nine years old before we develop the capabilities of complex, abstract and rational thought. But, by then, we have already assimilated and incorporated many Deep Identity factors, including:
- Culture (including race and ethnicity)

- Language

- Religion

- Class

- Gender

Not all aspects of our identity are a part of our deep Identity. However, the core basics that are part of our deep identity don't change easily. Virtually no one, for example, can change their racial identity. It is only with great difficulty (and several operations) that a person can change their sex. The transition from poverty class to middle class can be accomplished without an operation — but it isn't easy. The lines keeping us in our cultural or ethnic group, class status and religion are, at most, only slightly flexible, if at all.

Because deep identity develops <u>before</u> rational thought, we treat it NOT as an aspect of identity, but as REALITY. Our Deep Identity tends to be our definition of reality. Therefore, changing aspects of our deep identity means changing a part of ourselves that was formed before we were conscious of ourselves as individuals. Changing deep identity means leaving behind a core part of one's self — that which we accept as reality. This is easier said than done.

A threat to one or more aspects of our Deep Identity is a threat to our core identity. We take it very personally — and, generally, very non-rationally.

EXERCISE: **Experiencing Deep Identity**

1. Deep Identity and Commonality:

     a. What are your "Deep Identities"? (Write them down...)

     b. What are your facilitators? (Write them down...)

     c. Where are the commonalities?

     d. Where are the differences?

2. Of the five aspects of deep identity:

     a. Which ones are most powerful for you?

     b. Least powerful?

3. Have you had the experience of being a minority in your "deep identities"?

     a. Was the experience positive? Negative?

     b, How did you feel?

4. How does "Deep Identity" affect the development of community?

6.3 **What Is Deep Conflict?**

There are many different types or flavors of conflict and discord:

- I can argue with my sister.

- Someone takes my parking space or cuts me off in traffic.

- We fight over casting our political ballots.

- Someone is passed over for a job because of their age (too old or too young).

- I'm not chosen for a sports team because I'm not fast enough or strong enough.

These can be very serious matters, the type of discord and conflict that leads to hurt feelings, broken marriages and even violence.

Although this type of conflict is serious, there is a deeper level, another type of conflict and discord:

- Members of a different religion burn down the houses of everyone who shares my religion.

- I am beaten by a person of a different race.

- Members of an ethnic minority group are blocked from voting due to bureaucratic regulations.

- I am denied economic opportunity because of the style of my clothes, my haircut, or my beard.

- People with different languages go to war with each other.

There is a qualitative difference between the two sets of examples. All are conflicts, but the second type is more likely to lead to lasting conflict. Those are deep conflicts — conflicts based on deep identity factors. While all conflicts are painful, it is the nature of deep conflict that leads to violence, deep hatred, long-term discord and war.

Deep Conflicts are the situations where we are LEAST LIKELY to practice the Golden Rule.

6.4 The Roots of Deep Conflict?

Therefore, we come to a definition of Deep Conflict: Deep Conflict consists of opposition to our Deep Identity and stems from a threat to the following factors:

- Race, ethnicity and/or culture

- Language

- Class

- Religion

- Gender

Of course, threats to physical existence are the deepest of deep identity factors. However, because it is so fundamental (to every living organism), it is omitted from this list of very human factors.

Why not include other known aspects of conflict and discrimination in deep conflict? Aspects like:

- Sexual preference

- Age or generationism

- Regionalism

- Nationality

These, of course, are important issues. However, these issues are not aspects of deep identity:

- They are not a part of every human's genetic makeup.

- They are not a foundational aspect of virtually every human culture.

- They are not learned by every human from parents and their community.

- They have not formed the basis of centuries-long conflicts.

- They are not the basis of the more than 70 wars raging on our planet right now.

If we are going to transform ourselves and transform our society, we must take on the toughest, most intractable issues, the ones that threaten our existence as humans on this planet. If we can resolve Deep Conflict, we can create a climate where the other issues can be successfully addressed. On the other hand, if we do not resolve Deep Conflicts, we will never be able to create a world that works for all beings.

6.5 How NOT to Resolve Deep Conflict

Deep Conflict is held at the most base, fundamental level within each of us. Therefore, typical conflict resolution, which relies on people behaving rationally and being able to perceive their own best interests, does not adequately address the deep conflict issues.

Forced separation: The traditional approach to resolving deep conflict is to separate the conflicting parties. There is little evidence that this works. There is abundant evidence that it doesn't. At best, separation produces a temporary truce—at worst, it bundles the sparks with the fuel for the next conflagration.

There have been 50 years of religious and political separation between India and Pakistan, but no end to their conflict, which now threatens to go nuclear. Similar issues in Korea, the former Yugoslavia, Cyprus, the Middle East and many other places demonstrate that separation does not end deep conflict.

Forced integration: Forcing people together doesn't work either! Forcing people together can be interpreted as a threat to Deep Identity – a threat to one's REALITY. When one of the conflicting parties is doing the forcing, it can be interpreted as cultural superiority and/or imperialism. Trying to force integration in America has not led to whites and blacks ending the difficulties produced by centuries of slavery and apartheid. Nor did forced integration end Deep Conflict with Native Americans and white Americans (Indian Schools) or Egyptian Christians and Muslims. In many instances, the forced integration has led to a deeper, more insidious form of self-apartheid.

People resist both tendencies. People are afraid of being separated because they fear the isolation may decrease their power and increase hatred and the propensity for violence and war. People are afraid of being forced together because they fear losing their identities.

6.6 How Deep Conflict Is Resolved

So, if neither separation nor integration works, what does?

Commonway has evidence-based approaches to resolving deep conflict by addressing Deep Identity. These methodologies include:

- Acknowledging Deep Identity, then Inviting Adversaries to Transcend Deep Conflict

- Transcending Deep Conflict without Destroying Deep Identity — The Two-Step Commonway Process

- Using Proximity to Transcend Deep Conflict

6.6.1 Acknowledging Deep Identity, then Inviting Adversaries to Transcend Deep Conflict

People cling tenaciously to their deep identities—until invited (or required) to transcend them. Sometimes, the invitation takes the form of a threat to all identities. For example, in the aftermath of an earthquake, hurricane or other overwhelming and mutually defined threat, people reach out to each other across the previously existing lines of division. At that point, deep identity aspects don't matter. Or, they are superseded by the deepest identity, self-preservation.

History is replete with examples of people risking their lives to rescue others from disaster — not only complete strangers, but people of different religion, race or culture.

In the aftermath of the San Francisco earthquake, people of different races and classes came together to rescue each other. In the aftermath of the Portland flood of 1996, thousands of ordinary Portlanders rallied to protect downtown Portland by sandbagging (but did not work to save the houses of the rich).

In the aftermath of the 2004 Indian Ocean tsunami, both the soldiers of the Government of Sri Lanka and the LTTE ("Tamil Tigers") cooperated with each other in helping displaced citizens. Their cooperation lasted so long, they had to be ORDERED by their respective leaders to go back to killing each other!

6.6.2 Transcending Deep Conflict without Destroying Deep Identity — The Two-Step Commonway Process

In the Commonway experience, combining BOTH the separation and integration strategies creates the best chance for transcending Deep Conflict. We do this by first separating people into single-focus stakeholder groups (separation) and then bringing them back together in inter-community dialogs (integration).

Honoring Deep Identity through Separation: We invite people into affinity groups where they will be most comfortable. They are invited to explore their issues in a facilitated dialog that invites them to expand beyond narrow, separatist thinking. Participants know in advance that the purpose of the single-focus affinity group dialog is to prepare for integrated dialog.

Many times, the single-focus groups allow participants to "blow off steam" in a way that is not damaging to the Other. This allows participants to see and articulate the real issues.

Honoring Deep Identity through Integration: We invite people to transcend their barriers, but to do so in a way that leaves the Deep Identity factors intact and unthreatened. Our task is not to erase difference (especially with regard to the important and fragile deep identities), but to make barriers permeable, not hard and exclusivist.

6.6.3 Proximity Transcends Deep Conflict

To transcend Deep Conflict, we rely on something that is so deeply ingrained in humans that it may be genetic: people in physical proximity to each other tend to transcend Deep Conflict. There is ample evidence that this happens:

- Two heart cells, from two different people, will pulse in rhythm when brought into proximity with each other.

- Women who share living or working space will synchronize their menstrual cycles.

- Men and women in an army unit will bond with each other, even across race, language or class. This bond does not necessarily extend to other units of the same army, showing that the bond has to do with proximity.

There are factors that can make the bond happen faster by having the parties (in order of importance):

1. Using an inclusive, neutral convener/ facilitator/advocate who assembles the parties and keeps order: "The Advocate of the Whole." The convener can be a member of one of the groups in conflict, as long as he/ she can transcend their membership and truly be present for the whole.

2. Everyone inhabiting the same room (not video conferencing).

3. Eating and drinking while in each other's presence. This is a very important point! Something happens when eating and drinking in each other's presence. It does not have to be more than snacks and coffee.

4. Being within touching distance but without actually touching, which can be threatening or forbidden for some cultures. (Sitting at a table small enough to reach across and shake hands.)

5. Working on some task or assignment in common, one that does not have people focusing on their conflicts. (We call this "The Magnet.")

6. Working on an easy task, before facing more difficult ones, for example, having a table arrange their children and grandchildren in chronological order.

7. Facing each other.

8. Talking to each other, not using spokespersons or representatives.

There are also factors that will retard or destroy this process:

- Throwing people together, without guidance, facilitation or direction.

- Convening only hardliners, people who are committed to extremist positions and the existence of conflict.

- Putting one group in a favored or controlling position over others.

- Giving the parties a task or activity that focuses their attention on their conflicts or differences before they have eaten together, before they become acquainted with each other, etc.

In this process, we have helped people to connect with each other WITHOUT asking them to give up their deep identities.. Our goal is to have them leave the room with their deep identities still in place, but with their deep barriers made more permeable.

Commonway's process to build deep connection brings people into the same room, then facilitates the natural bonding process. Commonway has developed several tools to facilitate this process including the Commons Café. (See the Commonway web pages on the Commons Café.)

EXERCISE: **Transcending Deep Conflict**

1. Do your current communities include people with different "deep identities" from yours?

2. Have you tried to include people with different "deep identities" into your current communities?

      a. What was the result?

3. What are your experiences with "deep conflict" (conflicts based on "deep identity")?
      a. Have you ever been excluded because of any of your "deep identities"?

      b. How did it feel?

      c. How did you resolve it?

4. Have you ever excluded others, based on their "deep identities"? How do you believe your "other" felt? (If you answer "no" to this question, please think again. Exclusion can be subtle):
      a. Omitting someone from an event because you determine "they probably won't like it";

      b. Leaving someone out of an event because of their language;

      c. Not inviting someone because "their religion probably will not allow them to participate".

5. What are your experiences with healing "deep conflict"?

6. What are your experiences with making a "deep connection"?

LEARNING DISCUSSION OF CHAPTER SIX

Consult your journal before answering these questions:

For Each Section:

- What was one thing you agreed with?

- What was one thing you didn't understand, or you disagreed with?

For Each Exercise:

- What was your experience of the exercise?

- What did you learn? What will you take away?

- What did you find unclear or difficult?

For the Chapter:

- What was your strongest take-away from this chapter?

- What was your most difficult or challenging concept to practice?

- What was the most interesting thing you wrote after your meditation?

MEDITATION
Reflections on Your Personal Journey
Conclude this chapter with a five- to ten-minute
meditation. Record your reflections in your
journal or below.

THE INCLUSIVITY PRAYER

At the end of in-person and online sessions of "Practicing Inclusivity", the group recites this "Inclusivity Prayer". We invite you to do so here, even if you are a group of one. This is a prayer that does not require a religious doctrine — the atheists in our groups have no trouble in reciting it.

While this is a prayer that encompasses all living beings, it starts with you. Once you are whole, secure and balanced, you can bring wholeness, security and balance to others.

In the second part, picture in your mind/heart a person with whom you find it very easy to practice inclusivity. Then, next time, picture in your mind/heart a person with whom you find it very difficult to practice inclusivity.

In the third part, picture in your mind/heart all living beings, and the Earth as a living being.

MAY I BE WELL.

MAY I BE SECURE.

MAY I BE HAPPY.

MAY YOU BE WELL.

MAY YOU BE SECURE.

MAY YOU BE HAPPY.

MAY ALL BEINGS BE WELL.

MAY ALL BEINGS BE SECURE.

MAY ALL BEINGS BE HAPPY.

And so it is.

CPSIA information can be obtained
at www.ICGtesting.com
Printed in the USA
LVHW06s1335171018
593914LV00027B/347/P

9 781517 347819